COLORADO

EXPLORE THE UNITED STATES

Sarah Tieck

Big Buddy BOOKS

Explore the United States

VISIT US AT
www.abdopublishing.com

Published by ABDO Publishing Company, PO Box 398166, Minneapolis, MN 55439.

Copyright © 2013 by Abdo Consulting Group, Inc. International copyrights reserved in all countries. No part of this book may be reproduced in any form without written permission from the publisher. Big Buddy Books™ is a trademark and logo of ABDO Publishing Company.

Printed in the United States of America, North Mankato, Minnesota.
022012
092012

 PRINTED ON RECYCLED PAPER

Coordinating Series Editor: Rochelle Baltzer
Contributing Editors: Megan M. Gunderson, BreAnn Rumsch, Marcia Zappa
Graphic Design: Adam Craven
Cover Photograph: *Shutterstock*: gary yim.
Interior Photographs/Illustrations: *AP Photo*: AP Photo (p. 23), Eric Bakke (p. 25), Jack Dempsey (p. 26), Lenny Ignelzi (p. 25), North Wind Picture Archives via AP Images (p. 13); *Glow Images*: Arco Images (p. 30); *iStockphoto*: iStockphoto.com/creighton359 (p. 30), iStockphoto.com/EdgeofReason (p. 9), iStockphoto.com/gladassfanny (p. 27), iStockphoto.com/kjschoen (p. 30), iStockphoto.com/Missing35mm (p. 17), iStockphoto.com/narawon (pp. 21, 26), iStockphoto.com/smithcjb (p. 9), iStockphoto.com/SWKrullimaging (p. 5); *Shutterstock*: Linda Armstrong (p. 19), John Hoffman (p. 27), Phillip Lange (p. 30), Theresa Martinez (p. 27), Photography Perspectives-Jeff Smith (p. 17), Neil Podoll (p. 11), John S. Sfondilias (p. 29).

All population figures taken from the 2010 US census.

Library of Congress Cataloging-in-Publication Data

Tieck, Sarah, 1976-
  Colorado / Sarah Tieck.
    p. cm. -- (Explore the United States)
  ISBN 978-1-61783-344-1
  1. Colorado--Juvenile literature. I. Title.
  F776.3.T54 2012
  978.8--dc23
                                2012000754

COLORADO

Contents

ONE NATION

The United States is a **diverse** country. It has farmland, cities, coasts, and mountains. Its people come from many different backgrounds. And, its history covers more than 200 years.

Today the country includes 50 states. Colorado is one of these states. Let's learn more about Colorado and its story!

Did You Know?

Colorado became a state on August 1, 1876. It was the thirty-eighth state to join the nation.

Garden of the Gods is a park in
Colorado. It has unusual rock formations.

5

COLORADO UP CLOSE

The United States has four main **regions**. Colorado is in the West.

Colorado has six states on its borders. Wyoming is to the north. Nebraska is northeast, and Kansas is east. Oklahoma and New Mexico are south. And, Utah is west.

Colorado has a total area of 104,095 square miles (269,605 sq km). More than 5 million people live in the state.

REGIONS OF THE UNITED STATES

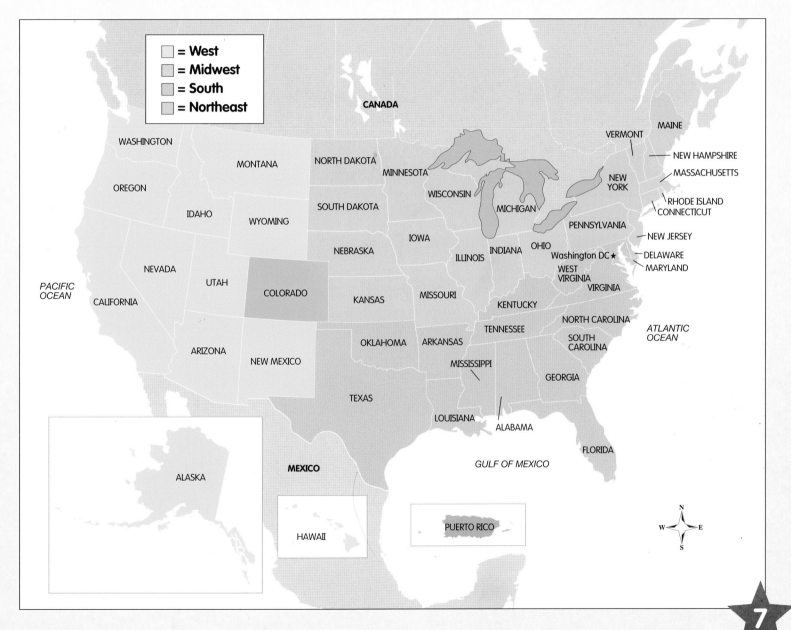

= West
= Midwest
= South
= Northeast

CANADA

WASHINGTON
MONTANA
NORTH DAKOTA
MINNESOTA
VERMONT
MAINE
NEW HAMPSHIRE
MASSACHUSETTS
OREGON
WISCONSIN
NEW YORK
RHODE ISLAND
CONNECTICUT
IDAHO
SOUTH DAKOTA
WYOMING
MICHIGAN
PENNSYLVANIA
NEW JERSEY
IOWA
OHIO
DELAWARE
MARYLAND
NEBRASKA
INDIANA
Washington DC★
NEVADA
ILLINOIS
WEST VIRGINIA
VIRGINIA
UTAH
PACIFIC OCEAN
COLORADO
KANSAS
MISSOURI
KENTUCKY
CALIFORNIA
TENNESSEE
NORTH CAROLINA
ATLANTIC OCEAN
ARIZONA
OKLAHOMA
ARKANSAS
SOUTH CAROLINA
NEW MEXICO
MISSISSIPPI
GEORGIA
TEXAS
LOUISIANA
ALABAMA
FLORIDA
GULF OF MEXICO
ALASKA
MEXICO
HAWAII
PUERTO RICO

N
W   E
S

7

IMPORTANT CITIES

Denver is the **capital** of Colorado. It is also the state's largest city, with 600,158 people.

Denver is near the base of the Rocky Mountains. It is sometimes called the "Mile High City." That's because it is one mile (1.6 km) above sea level.

8

COLORADO

Denver ★● Aurora

● Colorado Springs

The US Mint in Denver makes coins. If the letter *D* is stamped on a coin, that means it was made in Denver.

The Rocky Mountains are just west of Denver.

Colorado Springs is Colorado's second-largest city. It is home to 416,427 people. This city is located at the foot of the Rocky Mountains. Several military bases are there, as well as the US Air Force Academy.

Aurora is the third-largest city in the state. Its population is 325,078. This city is near Denver. It is close to Denver International Airport.

Did You Know?

Pikes Peak is located near Colorado Springs. It is 14,110 feet (4,301 m) tall.

Colorado Springs is known for being sunny. It has about 300 sunny days each year!

Colorado in History

Colorado's history includes Native Americans and settlers. Beginning in the 1500s, the Spanish explored present-day Colorado. Native Americans had lived there for many years.

Over time, more people explored and settled the land. In 1858, gold was found near Denver. Then, many people came in search of more gold. In 1861, Colorado became a territory. It became a state in 1876.

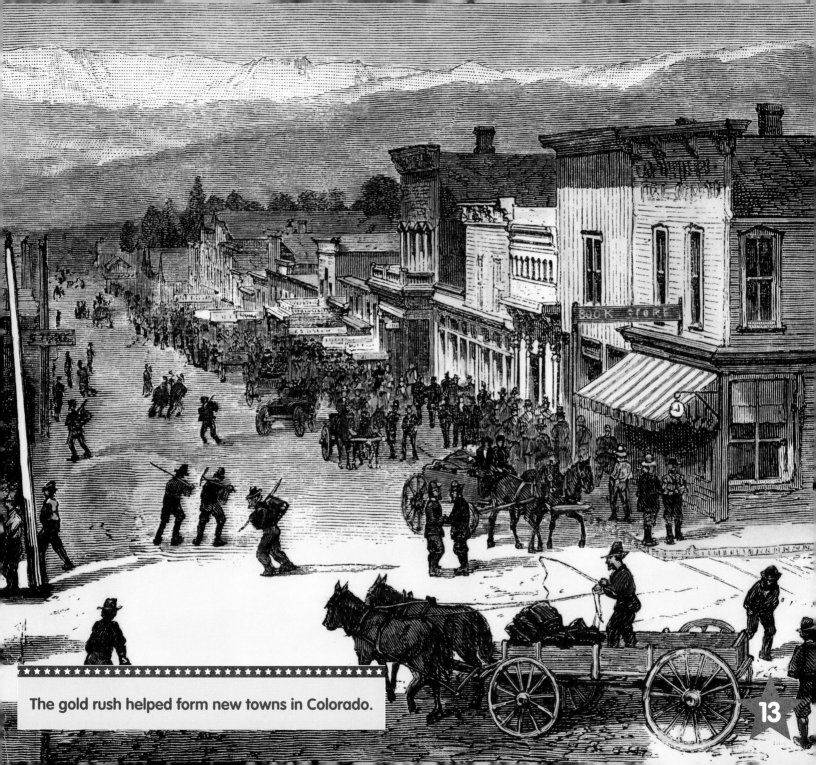

The gold rush helped form new towns in Colorado.

13

Timeline

1806

American explorer Zebulon Pike entered the Colorado area and found a tall mountain peak. The peak was later named Pikes Peak after him.

1858

Gold was found at Dry Creek, near what is now Denver.

1893

Katharine Lee Bates wrote the words to the song "America the Beautiful." She had been inspired by the view from the top of Pikes Peak.

1906

The US Mint in Denver made its first coins.

1800s

1861

The Colorado Territory was created. In 1867, Denver became its **capital**.

1876

Colorado became the thirty-eighth state on August 1.

1893

Colorado voted to allow women to vote. That was 27 years before the whole country allowed this.

14

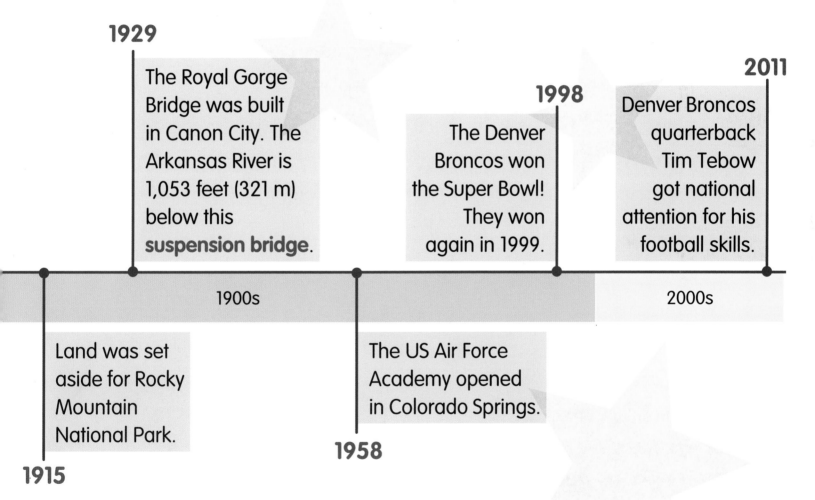

1929

The Royal Gorge Bridge was built in Canon City. The Arkansas River is 1,053 feet (321 m) below this **suspension bridge**.

2011

Denver Broncos quarterback Tim Tebow got national attention for his football skills.

1998

The Denver Broncos won the Super Bowl! They won again in 1999.

1900s

2000s

Land was set aside for Rocky Mountain National Park.

The US Air Force Academy opened in Colorado Springs.

1915

1958

ACROSS THE LAND

Colorado has forests, mountains, **plateaus**, **canyons**, and **plains**. The Rocky Mountains run through central Colorado. The state also has many lakes and rivers. The Colorado River flows through northern Colorado.

Many types of animals make their homes in Colorado. These include mountain goats, coyotes, and beavers.

★ **Did You Know?**

Colorado's weather changes with the seasons. Denver's average July temperature is about 72°F (22°C). In January, it is about 30°F (-1°C).

★★★★★★★★★★★★★★★★★★★★★★★★★★

Bighorn sheep (*left*) and elk (*below*) live in Colorado's mountains.

Earning a Living

Colorado has important businesses in mining, farming, manufacturing, and **telecommunications**. They provide jobs for people in Colorado.

Some people have jobs helping visitors to the state. Many people visit Colorado for vacation. They often ski, hike, or do other outdoor activities.

Did You Know?

Cattle are an important product raised in Colorado. They provide food for people.

Hay is one of Colorado's main crops. It is grown throughout the state.

NATURAL WONDER

The Rocky Mountains, or Rockies, form the largest mountain chain in North America. They stretch more than 3,000 miles (4,800 km) from Alaska to New Mexico. In some places, the Rockies are more than 300 miles (480 km) wide!

Rocky Mountain National Park is in northern Colorado. People visit the park to hike, fish, and rock climb. Many animals live in the park. These include deer, mountain lions, black bears, and moose.

The Bear Lake area is a popular hiking spot in Rocky Mountain National Park.

HOMETOWN HEROES

Many famous people have lived in Colorado. M. Scott Carpenter was born in Boulder in 1925. He was one of the first US astronauts.

In 1962, Carpenter circled Earth three times in *Aurora 7*. He was the second American to circle Earth in a spaceship! Carpenter also explored the sea. In 1965, he visited the ocean floor to do experiments.

Carpenter flew in *Aurora 7* for nearly five hours. The spaceship landed in the Atlantic Ocean.

John Elway was born in 1960 in Washington state. He was a famous quarterback for the Denver Broncos football team. He played from 1983 to 1999.

Elway became known for his play in a 1987 game. He led his team on a 98-yard drive and threw a touchdown that tied the game! Later, Elway helped the Broncos win the 1998 and 1999 Super Bowls.

In 2011, Elway became an executive for the Broncos. He helps oversee the team's operations.

The 1998 Super Bowl was the first one the Broncos had won! Elway (*center*) was a star player.

Tour Book

Do you want to go to Colorado? If you visit the state, here are some places to go and things to do!

 **View**

Walk across the Royal Gorge Bridge. It is the world's highest suspension bridge!

 Cheer

See the Denver Broncos play football at Sports Authority Field at Mile High Stadium.

 Ski

Take to the famous, snowy slopes of Aspen or Vail! Famous skiers, such as Lindsey Vonn, have trained there.

 Remember

Visit Mesa Verde National Park and see Cliff Palace. Native Americans built a community into a cliff about 800 years ago.

 Explore

Stop by the US Air Force Academy near Colorado Springs. People train there to become Air Force pilots!

A Great State

The story of Colorado is important to the United States. The people and places that make up this state offer something special to the country. Together with all the states, Colorado helps make the United States great.

Great Sand Dunes National Park and Preserve is in Colorado. It is home to North America's tallest sand dunes. Some rise more than 700 feet (200 m)!

Fast Facts

Date of Statehood:
August 1, 1876

Population (rank):
5,029,196
(22nd most-populated state)

Total Area (rank):
104,095 square miles
(8th largest state)

Motto:
"Nil Sine Numine"
(Nothing Without Providence)

Nickname:
Centennial State

State Capital:
Denver

Flag:

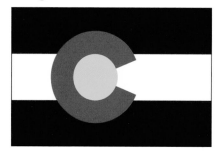

Flower: White and Lavender Columbine

Postal Abbreviation:
CO

Tree: Colorado Blue Spruce

Bird: Lark Bunting

Important Words

canyon a long, narrow valley between two cliffs.

capital a city where government leaders meet.

diverse made up of things that are different from each other.

plains flat or rolling land without trees.

plateau (pla-TOH) a raised area of flat land.

region a large part of a country that is different from other parts.

suspension bridge a bridge that has its roadway hanging from cables.

telecommunications the business of sending messages by electronic means, such as telephone or computer.

Web Sites

To learn more about Colorado, visit ABDO Publishing Company online. Web sites about Colorado are featured on our Book Links page. These links are routinely monitored and updated to provide the most current information available.

www.abdopublishing.com

Index